Checker zoo

The Number of Players: 2

The Object of the Game: To score the most points by getting your playing pieces on the opponent's high-numbered squares.

The Playing Pieces: Each player needs 12 identical playing pieces that are different from his or her opponent's. For example, you can use red and black checker pieces, doughnut-shaped and square cereal pieces, or dark and light buttons.

The Play: To begin, each player lines up playing pieces on the numbered spaces on his or her side of the board. The younger player goes first.

As in checkers, each player takes turns moving diagonally across the board. A move can be just one space, or the player may jump over and capture one or more of the opponent's playing pieces. Unlike checkers, however, the object of the game is not to capture all your opponent's pieces.

The Winner: When one player has pieces on each of the opponent's four "number 10" squares, the play stops. Each player figures out his or her points by adding up the number of his or her opponent's squares on which he or she has pieces. The person with the higher score wins.

Math Concepts: Logical reasoning.
Adding 10's, 5's, and 3's.
Comparing numbers to see who has the higher score.

I LOVE MATH

THE CASE
OF THE
MISSING

ZEBRA STRIPES

ZOO MATH

TIME
LIFE for
Children™

ALEXANDRIA, VIRGINIA

ALL ABOUT I LOVE MATH!

Help solve a height riddle on page 18.

Dear Parent,

The *I Love Math* series shows children that math is all around them in everything they do. It can be found at the grocery store, at a soccer game, in the kitchen, at the zoo, even in their own bodies. As you collect this series, each book will fill in another piece of your child's world, showing how math is a natural part of everyday activities.

What Is Math?

Math is much more than manipulating numbers; the goal of math education today is to help children become problem solvers. This means teaching kids to observe the world around them by looking for patterns and relationships, estimating, measuring, comparing, and using reasoning skills. From an early age, children do this naturally. They divide up cookies to share with friends, recognize shapes in pizza, measure how tall they have grown, or match colors and patterns as they dress themselves. Young children love math. But when math only takes the form of abstract formulas on worksheets, children begin to dislike it. The *I Love Math* series is designed to keep math natural and appealing.

Guess how long I am. Measure me and find out on page 22.

How Do Children Learn Math?

Research has shown that children learn best by doing. Therefore, *I Love Math* is a hands-on, interactive learning experience. The math concepts are woven into stories in which entertaining characters invite your child to help them solve math challenges. Activities reinforce the concepts, and parent notes offer ways you and your child can have more fun with this program.

We have worked closely with math educators to include in these books a full range of math skills. As the series progresses, repetition of these skills in different formats will help your child master the basics of mathematical thinking.

What Will You Find in *Zoo Math*?
In *Zoo Math* your child will learn that math can be found even at the zoo. He or she will use estimation to count a flock of flamingos; graphing to compare the different heights of giraffes; classification to determine the identity of some mysterious animals; and logical thinking to help rescue a little mouse from riddling animals in the rain forest.

As you read the book with your child, take the time to discuss the stories and the math in them. At the bottom of many pages there are hints or questions in italics that encourage discussion. To get the most out of the book, read the stories more than once. Each time you read them you will discover something new!

We hope you and your child will have fun with *Zoo Math* and both say:

I LOVE MATH!

The Editors
Time-Life for Children

Help! We're losing our stripes! Find out why on page 28!

Table of Contents

Go, Go, Go Flamingo 6

ESTIMATION: LARGER NUMBERS

Identify a range of numbers to guess how many
flamingos are in a picture. Also explore multiplication.

Just Like Us 8

LOGICAL THINKING: CLASSIFICATION

Use clues about a mysterious new
zoo animal to identify it.

Throw It Out! 17

LOGICAL THINKING: CLASSIFICATION

Explore the relationships among groups of zoo animals and numbers.

Why Does a Giraffe Make a Graph? 18

STATISTICS: GRAPHS

Find out how making a graph helps hungry giraffes
get their food. Also compare heights of the herd of giraffes.

Stringing Along 22

MEASUREMENT: LENGTH

Use string to find out the lengths of a snake,
two birds, and several lizards. Also use estimation.

The Case of the Missing Zebra Stripes 28

MEASUREMENT: TIME

Explore time to the hour by noting how a detective
uses a time pattern to help solve a mystery at the zoo.
Also use statistics and logical thinking.

Monkey With a Minute 38

MEASUREMENT: TIME
Experience a minute by timing several humorous activities.
Also learn a way of timing a minute without a clock.

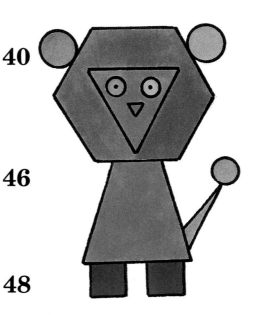

Leo the Line 40

GEOMETRY: LINES AND SHAPES
Investigate the properties of lines by following
the antics of a talking line and its friends.
Also recognize shapes.

Line Up 46

GEOMETRY: LINES AND SHAPES
Learn an easy way to draw several shapes
by following a lion's directions.

Henry's Tale 48

LOGICAL THINKING: DRAWING CONCLUSIONS

COMPUTATION: ADDITION, SUBTRACTION, AND MULTIPLICATION
Use logic and compuation skills to help rescue an inquisitive mouse.
Also explore place value.

Rain Forest Riddles 58

LOGICAL THINKING: DRAWING CONCLUSIONS

MEASUREMENT: TIME,MONEY
Use mathematical reasoning to answer riddles.

How Does an Alligator Use a Calculator? 60

COMPUTATION: ADDITION AND SUBTRACTION
Find the missing numbers as an alligator
takes a census of the zoo.

Calculator Code 62

COMPUTATION: ADDITION AND SUBTRACTION
Use a calculator and a number code to explore the
values of larger numbers. Also use estimation and a code.

GO, GO, GO FLAMINGO
About how many flamingos are in this picture?

Are there between 10 and 20?

MORE FUN. Next time you are at the grocery store, have your child estimate how many loaves of bread or cans of soup are on a shelf.

ANSWERS. There are approximately 130 flamingos in the picture. Of the number ranges suggested, "between 100 and 200" is correct. There would be 200 legs in the air.

Just Like Us

One dark night, a family of mysterious animals arrived at the gates of the City Zoo looking for a home. Listen to the clues and help the zoo keeper figure out who these animals are.

MATH FOCUS: LOGICAL THINKING—CLASSIFICATION. By classifying things, children make comparisons, a skill necessary for problem solving.

As you read the story to your child, discuss what the different groups of animals have in common.

What do all of these animals have in common?

MORE FUN. Have your child gather about 10 toys, sort them into groups according to similar characteristics, and tell how the toys in each group are alike.

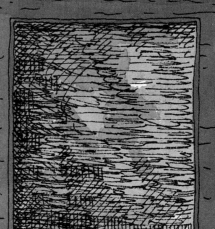

What do all of these have in common?

What do all of these have in common?

13

otter

platypus

frog

swan

spoonbill

beaver

raccoon

monkey

Which animal lays eggs and
has hair, webbed feet, a bill,
and a flat tail?

15

Throw it out!

One of these animals is not like the others.

Which one is it?

Throw it out!

Which one doesn't belong?

Why?

Throw it out!

Which number is different? Throw it out!

10	11
20	30

Throw one out!

1 + 1	2 + 2
3 + 3	1 + 3

17

MATH FOCUS: LOGICAL THINKING— CLASSIFICATION. By classifying things, children make comparisons, a skill necessary for solving problems.

MORE FUN. Have your child name four objects or numbers—three that have something in common and one that is different—and challenge family members to tell which one doesn't belong. Ask your child to explain why.

Why does a giraffe make a graph?

In a most modern manner
A famous zoo planner
Built a place where giraffes could have fun.
Soon giraffes of all ages
Were moved from their cages
And started to play and to run.

But no one could reach
The food, except Keach.
The platform was simply too high.
The shorter ones grumbled
As their stomachs rumbled,
And the little ones started to cry.

Said the planner named Pete,
"Well, you all have to eat.
We won't go to sleep till it's right.
We will think of a plan
So each giraffe can
Have food at his or her height."

MATH FOCUS: STATISTICS. By using a bar graph, children learn to analyze information.

Have your child identify the giraffes on page 18 that are too short to reach the food. Help your child refer to the bar graph on page 20 when answering the questions in the poem.

Then said one giraffe,
"Let's make a bar graph
That will show you the
Heights of us all.
We'll all work together—
You can use your tape measure—
To find out who's short
And who's tall."

Pete measured each one,
And soon they were done.
Here are the heights they had then.
6 feet tall was fair Ella,
7 feet was Marbella,
And sweet Garibaldi was 10.

Keach was 16,
9 feet tall was Doreen,
13 feet tall was old Ben.
Billy was 7,
Peggy Sue was 11,
15 feet tall was young Ken.

MORE FUN. Take turns making up and answering questions about the giraffes by looking at the bar graph. Try questions such as, "How many feet taller is Ken than Billy? How many feet shorter than Ben is Ella?"

Who is the shortest?
And who is the tallest?
Who are the ones in between?
Whose heights are the same?
Can you say each one's name?
Now, that's really using your bean!

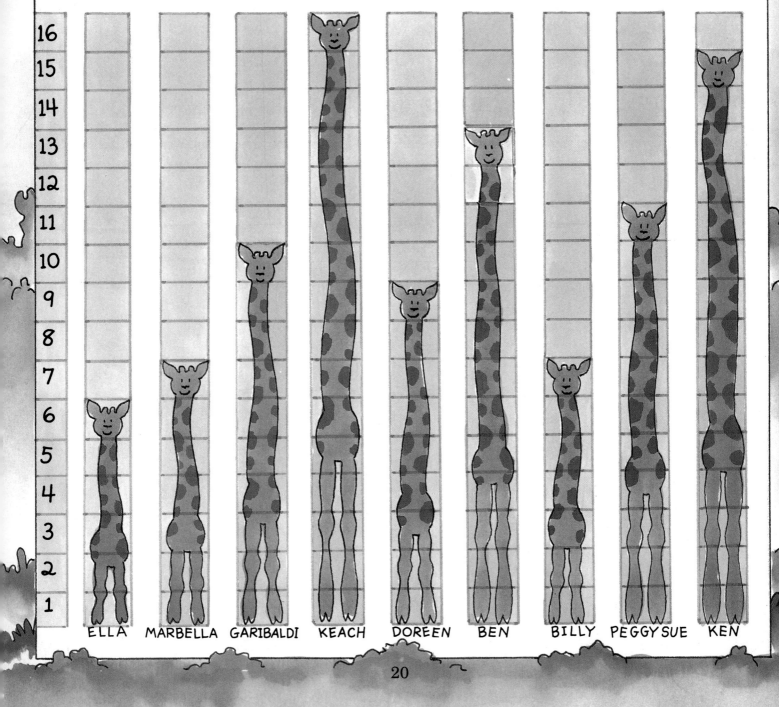

GIRAFFE GRAPH (HEIGHT IN FEET)

16 15 14 13 12 11 10 9 8 7 6 5 4 3 2 1

ELLA   MARBELLA   GARIBALDI   KEACH   DOREEN   BEN   BILLY   PEGGY SUE   KEN

What did this graph do?
Well, the crew at the zoo
Built 9 platforms made out of wood.
Now giraffes short and tall—
Giraffes one and all—
Reach their food the way
That they should.

About how many inches long am I?

0	1	2	3	4	5	6

↑ Start

Inches

MATH FOCUS: LENGTH—INCH. By estimating and then measuring the lengths of things, children get a real sense of how long things are.

22

Have available a pair of scissors and a long piece of string or yarn. Show your child how to use the ruler here correctly, by beginning any measurement at the "0."

First take a guess. Then use a piece of string to check.

Put one end of the string on the snake's head. Carefully lay the string on top of the snake's body until it goes from one end of the snake to the other.

Cut the string where it meets the end of the snake's tail.

Use the ruler to measure the length of the string.

Then tell the snake about how many inches long it is.

8   9   10   11   12

MORE FUN. Have your child estimate and then measure the lengths of several objects—for example, a pencil, a table, and a pet—or his or her height.

23

Your child can also draw each object and write its length in inches.

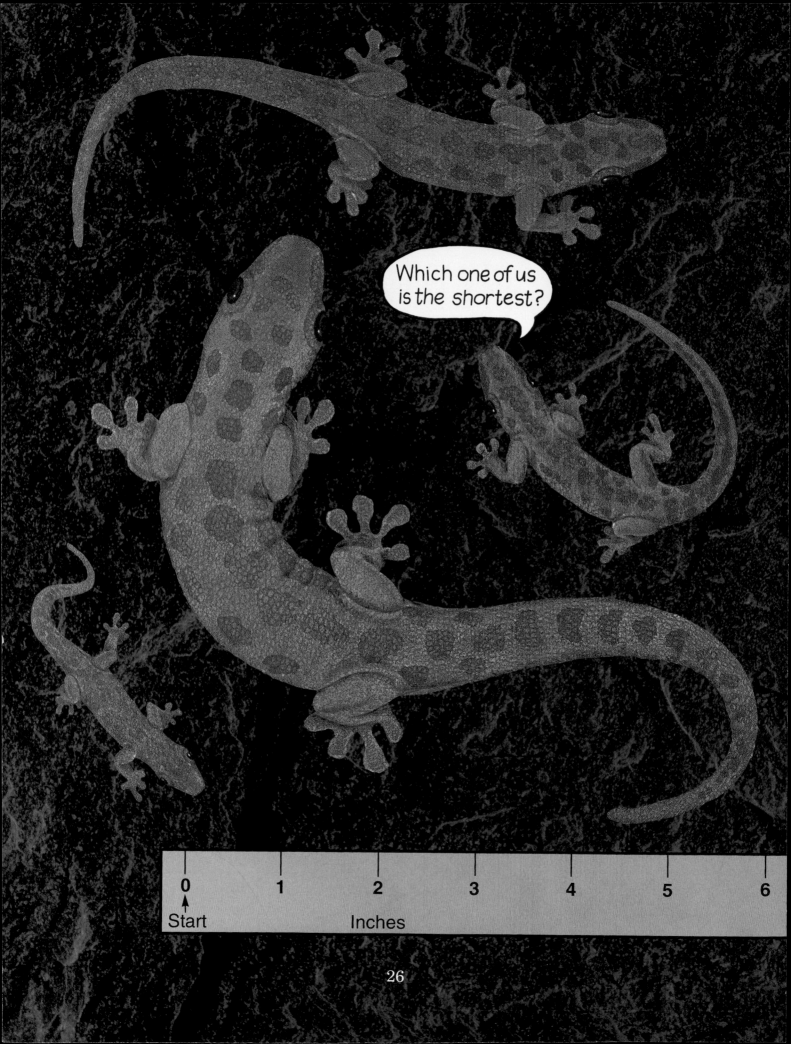

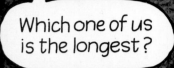

Which one of us is the longest?

Which two of us are about the same length?

Use your string.

7 8 9 10 11 12

The Case of the Missing Zebra Stripes

It was almost 11 o'clock on a sunny Thursday morning. Professor Guesser saw Willy Wallaby waiting for her at the zoo. "I came as fast as I could. What's the matter?" she asked.

"I have a terrible problem. I need your help. I'm afraid that the zebras are losing their stripes!" the zoo keeper exclaimed.

"Zebras losing their stripes? Are you sure?" asked Professor Guesser.

"I'm sure. When I fed the zebras at 6 o'clock last night, three of them had lost their stripes. Who will come to the zoo to see zebras with no stripes? What will I do?" sobbed Willy.

"There has to be an answer. I'll go with you to see the zebras. I'll keep a record of everything you do. Then I can work out what's going wrong," said Professor Guesser. "When do you check the zebras next?"

"Right now," said Willy.

MATH FOCUS: TIME—HOUR. By listening to a story about events that happen at certain times during the day, children become familiar with time to the hour.

28

Whenever specific times are mentioned in the story, point out the times shown on the clocks in the pictures.

Willy and the professor examined the herd of zebras. They finished at exactly 11:00. "Everything looks fine to me," said Professor Guesser, as she wrote the number zero on her chart. "No missing stripes here."

"But I'm sure I saw three zebras with missing stripes last night," said Willy.

"Perhaps time has something to do with it. I'll come back at 6:00 tonight and check them with you," said Professor Guesser.

In how many hours will the professor return to the zoo?

MORE FUN. Have your child make a chart of the times he or she eats meals over a couple of days and what he or she eats. Then have your child look for any patterns in the chart.

Willy and the professor returned to the zebra enclosure at 6 o'clock that evening. To Professor Guesser's amazement and to Willy Wallaby's horror, they saw three zebras with no stripes.

"This is so strange," said Professor Guesser. "None of the zebras were missing their stripes this morning. Now I see with my own eyes that they are indeed losing their stripes. What a mystery! Let me write this down on the chart I made."

"Do you have an answer?" asked Willy as he fed the zebras.

"Not yet," said the professor. "Solving problems takes time. I need to come back tomorrow for some more information."

PONY RIDES
10:00 - 5:00

HIPPOS

PONY RIDES
10:00 - 5:00

ELEPHANTS

SEALS

ZEBRAS

ZEBRAS WITH NO STRIPES		
DAY	TIME	NUMBER
THURSDAY	11:00	0
THURSDAY	6:00	3

On what day of the week will the professor return?

On Friday morning at 11 o'clock, they checked the zebras. And guess what—all of the zebras had their stripes again!

"I'm beginning to see a pattern here," said Professor Guesser. "Let's come back tonight at 6:00. I have an idea."

"What is it?" asked Willy excitedly.

"I'd rather not say until I'm sure, so you'll have to wait a little bit longer," said the professor.

ZEBRAS WITH NO STRIPES

DAY	TIME	NUMBER
THURSDAY	11:00	0
THURSDAY	6:00	3
FRIDAY	11:00	0

What do you think Willy and Professor Guesser will find at 6:00?

That night they returned to the zebra enclosure and found the same situation as the night before. Three of the zebras had no stripes.

"Have you figured out what's wrong?" asked Willy.

"Yes. Meet me tomorrow at the zebra enclosure an hour before you usually feed the zebras their dinner," said Professor Guesser.

"But I always feed them at 6 o'clock," said Willy Wallaby.

"I know. I know!" said Professor Guesser. "I'll see you tomorrow."

PONY RIDES
10:00 - 5:00

ZEBRAS WITH NO STRIPES		
DAY	TIME	NUMBER
THURSDAY	11:00	0
THURSDAY	6:00	3
FRIDAY	11:00	0
FRIDAY	6:00	3

At what time should Willy meet the professor tomorrow?

Can you figure out the solution to this mystery?

35

Willy Wallaby met Professor Guesser on Saturday afternoon at 5 o'clock.

"Hi, Willy," said Professor Guesser. "Quick! Count the zebras!"

"1, 2, 3, 4, 5, 6, 7, 8, 9, 10! There are 10 zebras," said Willy.

"Now, close your eyes and don't open them until I tell you to," said Professor Guesser. After a minute or two, she said, "OK, Willy, open your eyes and count the zebras again."

"1, 2, 3, 4, 5, 6, 7, 8, 9, 10, 11, 12, 13!" shrieked Willy, ". . . and 3 of them have no stripes! That's impossible! I'm going to faint."

"Don't faint, Willy! The zebras who lost their stripes never had any to begin with. They aren't really zebras; they're ponies," said Professor Guesser.

PONY RIDES
10:00-5:00

ZOO

36

Professor Guesser pointed to a sign by the pony ride. "Look," she said. "At 5 o'clock the ponies jumped over the low part of this fence into the zebra area. So at 6 o'clock, when you put out the food for the zebras, you saw 10 hungry zebras and 3 hungry ponies. That's why you thought you saw zebras with no stripes in the evening. After the ponies ate, they jumped back over the fence and had some of their own food."

"Those ponies sure do like to eat," said Willy. "I'll fix the fence, and make sure the ponies get more of their own food. Thank you, professor. You really solved my problem."

Professor Guesser laughed and said,
"No problem too great or too small—
Professor Guesser can solve them all!"

M·o·n·k·e·y w·i·t·h a M·i·n·u·t·e

18 19 20 21 22 23 24 25 26 27 28 29 30

17 16 15 14 13 12 11 10 9 8 7 6 5 4 3 2 1

When you tell someone to wait "just a minute," do you know how long that is? To find out, use a clock or a watch with a second hand. Start timing when the second hand is on any number. Stop timing when the second hand has gone all the way around and is back on the number it started on.

How long is a minute?

And this is how you can time a minute another way. Count up to 60 by saying "Mississippi" slowly after each number. Count like this: "1 Mississippi, 2 Mississippi, 3 Mississippi, 4 Mississippi"— all the way up to "60 Mississippi." Point to each number in the border as you count to 60.

Why do you count up to 60?

MATH FOCUS: TIME—MINUTE. By timing different activities for a minute, children increase their awareness of how long a moment of time is.

Have available a clock or a watch with a second hand, paper, and crayons. Time your child as he or she does each activity.

31 32 33 34 35 36 37 38 39 40 41 42 43

44
45
46
47
48
49
50
51
52
53
54
55
56
57
58
59
60

What can you do in a minute? First take a guess. Then have someone time you.

60

How many triangles can you draw in a minute?

Can you tie a pair of shoes in a minute?

Can you go to the kitchen, get a spoon, and come back in a minute?

HAPPY BIRTHDAY

How many times can you sing *Happy Birthday* in a minute?

Can you stand on one leg for a minute?

Can you draw 3 snowmen in a minute?

MORE FUN. Ask your child to think of other things that take a minute to do.

39

LEO THE LINE

MATH FOCUS: GEOMETRY—LINES AND SHAPES. By seeing how lines are used to create basic geometric forms, children develop geometric understanding and vocabulary. Help your child name each type of line and shape as it is introduced.

40

MORE FUN. Have your child draw a picture using thick, thin, straight, curved, intersecting, angled, and parallel lines.

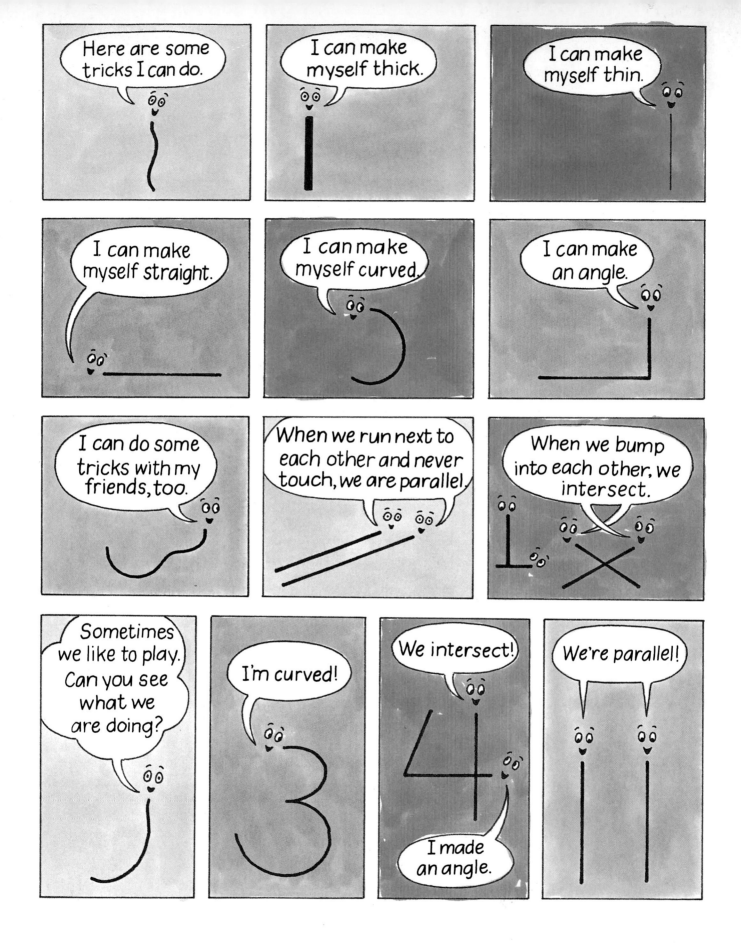

42

What shapes can you find
in this picture?

LINE UP

On your paper draw a straight line about the length of a new crayon.

Draw another straight line about the same length. Make it intersect the first line in the middle, like this.

Start at the end of one of the lines. Draw a line from it to the end of the next line.

Do this again and again and once again. Does the shape you drew look like any of the shapes I drew?

MATH FOCUS: GEOMETRY—LINES. By connecting the ends of intersecting lines, children learn how shapes are formed by a series of connecting lines.

Have available drawing paper and crayons.

Now draw three straight lines that intersect in the middle. Make them all about the same length.

Connect the ends of the lines. What shape did you draw?

Now draw eight straight lines that intersect in the middle.

Connect the ends of the lines. What shape did you draw?

MORE FUN. Have your child create more shapes by connecting other combinations of intersecting lines. You might also try making the lines uneven in length.

47

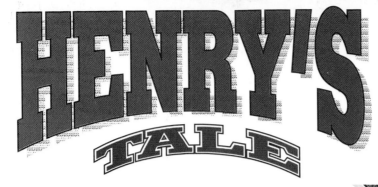

HENRY'S TALE

Henry was headed for the biggest adventure of his life, but he didn't know it.

"Hold on to Sylvia's tail, Henry," commanded his sister Judy as they walked toward the tiger area.

"You're not the boss," grumbled Henry. "I'm old enough to walk by myself!"

"But Granmousie is the boss," said Judy. "And she said we had to hold tails. You don't want to get lost, do you?"

"Humph! Holding tails is for babies," said Henry. "I'm old enough to take care of myself in this old zoo."

MATH FOCUS: LOGICAL THINKING, ADDITION, SUBTRACTION, AND MULTIPLICATION. By solving riddles, children learn to analyze information and to apply reasoning skills.

As you read the story, have your child describe what is happening in both the main pictures and in the "meanwhile" boxes.

THE Rain Forest EXHIBIT

!BEWARE!
RIDDLING
ANIMALS

Suddenly, Henry noticed an interesting sign in the distance. He walked toward it to get a closer look, and when he turned around he was all alone.

"Great!" thought Henry. "Now I can really have some fun." And he darted up the path toward a steep flight of stairs leading up to a sign. "I guess I'll see what's in there," Henry said to himself. As he pulled himself up the stairs he narrowly avoided being stepped on by a gigantic shoe.

As soon as he got inside, Henry felt warm wet air and saw lush green plants. And wonder of wonders, the ground was covered with sunflower seeds!

"Paradise!" said Henry as he gobbled the seeds.

"Rain forest!" corrected a raspy voice from above. "And you are eating my dinner."

M E A N W H I L E . . .

Down flew a macaw, landing with one huge foot on Henry's tail.

"I'm sorry. I didn't know the seeds were yours. Look, some are still here," apologized Henry.

"Hmm," said the macaw, not moving an inch. "I'll tell you what I'll do. If you can answer my riddle, I will let you go.

"I am thinking of two of these groups of sunflower seeds. The total number of seeds in the two groups is 10. One group has 2 more seeds than the other. Which two groups am I thinking of?"

What do you think the answer is?

MEANWHILE...

51

"Let's see," said Henry, who was petrified but tried not to show it. "I must find two amounts that add up to 10. Hmm. Well, 8 and 2 make 10."

Then Henry remembered what the macaw said—that one group must have 2 more seeds than the other. Henry said softly, "Well, it can't be 8 and 2 because the group of 8 has 6 more than the group of 2."

Henry spoke up. "I think it's the group with 6 seeds and the group with 4 seeds," he said with a shaking voice.

"You are right," said the macaw. "You may go on your way. Remember, in the rain forest, sunflower seeds are MINE."

"I'll remember," said Henry, and he ran up the nearest vine.

As he climbed up, Henry began to feel better. He could see all over the rain forest. He could see birds and trees and monkeys. MONKEYS?

M E A N W H I L E . . .

"Who's down there?" mumbled a low voice. "What's hanging on to my tail?"

"I can't see," mumbled another low voice. "Swing it over here, and I'll take a closer look at it."

"I'm not an *it,* I'm me!" called Henry in his loudest voice, as he swung back and forth. "Please stop swinging so I can get off."

"I'll stop swinging if you can answer my riddle," said the monkey with a mischievous smile.

"If 4 monkeys are swinging in the trees, and if twice as many monkeys are sleeping, how many monkeys are there in all?"

How many monkeys do you think there are in all?

53

"Oh, boy!" said Henry, still swinging back and forth. "Let me think. There are 4 monkeys swinging, and twice as many are sleeping. Hmm . . . two groups of 4 are 8—so there are 8 sleeping. Well, with 4 swinging and 8 sleeping, I know how many there are altogether! There are 12 monkeys in all," shouted Henry.

"That's right," said the monkey, and she let her tail down near a huge tree. Henry crept into the space between two roots and closed his eyes.

M E A N W H I L E . . .

"Think you're going to take a nap on my footstool, do you?" hissed a voice. "We'll see about that. Trespassing is serious business in the rain forest."

An Asian water dragon had a hind foot over the tree roots. She spread her toes apart just enough to let Henry peek out. "You must realize that trespassers must answer for their actions," hissed the dragon.

"You mean answer a riddle?" squeaked Henry.

"Exactly, and it's a hard one. Here it is," said the dragon.

"How old am I? I am younger than the number of months in a year. I am older than 8. Both digits in my age are the same."

How old do you think the dragon is?

55

"Let me think," said Henry to himself. "She's younger than the number of months in a year . . . now how many months are there in a year? Oh, I remember—12! So she's younger than 12. And she's older than 8. She must be 9, 10, or 11. Ah! The last part of the riddle says that both digits are the same. Now I know her age!"

Henry called out, "You're 11, aren't you?"

"Right," said the water dragon. "You're pretty smart—for a mouse. Hurry and go before I change my mind . . . ."

"I'm going. I'm going," said Henry as he hurried away toward the exit.

M E A N W H I L E . . .

As Henry hurried past the cayman pond, he saw the most wonderful sight in the world. "Granmousie!" called Henry. "Judy! Sylvia! Twinnies! Am I glad to see you! Where have you been?"

"It's a long story," said Granmousie. "Let's go home." She put her arms around him and held him tight, while the other mice danced around them in glee.

AND THIS IS THE END OF HENRY'S TALE

Rain Forest Riddles

APPLE LIME LEAF FIVE

What do I like to eat?
It has 4 letters.
It begins with the letter L.
It ends with the letter F.

This zoo opens at one of these times every morning. The opening time is half-past a certain hour. The zoo opens before 10:00. What time does the zoo open?

MATH FOCUS: LOGICAL THINKING, TIME, AND MONEY. To help your child solve these riddles, have available a pencil and paper, 5 quarters, 5 dimes, 5 nickels, and 5 pennies.

58

ICE CREAM

CHOCOLATE STRAWBERRY VANILLA

What is the entrance cost for children? It is more than 50¢ and less than 60¢. You use 5 of one coin and 1 of another to get this amount. You do not use any pennies.

ENTRANCE COSTS ADULTS 75¢ CHILDREN ▨¢

Sylvia, Judy, and Henry are getting ice cream. They all get different flavors. Sylvia does not get vanilla or chocolate. Judy does not get brown ice cream. What flavor of ice cream does each get?

MORE FUN. Have your child create his or her own riddles and challenge family members to solve them.

ANSWERS. The monkey likes to eat a leaf. The zoo opens at 9:30. The entrance cost for children is 55¢, using 5 dimes and 1 nickel. Sylvia gets strawberry ice cream, Judy gets vanilla, and Henry gets chocolate.

How does an alligator use a calculator?

The city zoo's administrator
Called for Percy Alligator.
"Our population has expanded.
Count them all!" the man demanded.

ALLIGATOR, ALLIGATOR! PUT IT ON YOUR CALCULATOR!

To do his job, the alligator
Used a hand-held calculator.
Quick reptilian computation
Found each total population.

ALLIGATOR, ALLIGATOR! PUT IT ON YOUR CALCULATOR!

A father and a mother bongo
Had a son and called him Pongo.
Parents 2, plus baby 1,
Makes how many bongos in the sun?

$2 + 1 = \square$

ALLIGATOR, ALLIGATOR! PUT IT ON YOUR CALCULATOR!

$3 + 6 = \square$

Bengal tigers, Oriental.
3 new cubs and 6 parental.
How many tigers in their cages,
Counting all, of any ages?

ALLIGATOR, ALLIGATOR! PUT IT ON YOUR CALCULATOR!

MATH FOCUS: ADDITION AND SUBTRACTION.
By completing number sentences to solve word
problems, children use problem-solving skills to
practice addition and subtraction. As you read
the poem, have your child point to each number
sentence and tell the missing number.

60

Monkeys swinging on a vine,
Parents 10 and babies 9.
So many monkeys joined the troop!
How many are there in this group?

$10 + 9 = \square$

ALLIGATOR, ALLIGATOR! PUT IT ON YOUR CALCULATOR!

8 big parrots brightly dressed,
Care for 2 chicks in their nest.
How many parrots perch in trees,
Doing bird activities?

$8 + 2 = \square$

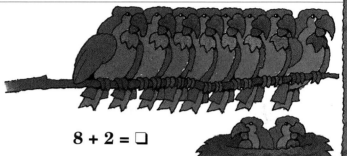

ALLIGATOR, ALLIGATOR! PUT IT ON YOUR CALCULATOR!

5 brown-spotted, tall giraffes,
Plus 3 brand-new, leggy calves.
How does Percy calculate
That the total now is 8?

$\square + \square = 8$

ALLIGATOR, ALLIGATOR! PUT IT ON YOUR CALCULATOR!

1 delighted Arctic fox
Had 4 kits inside a box.
What should Percy add to 1
To total 5 when he is done?

$1 + \square = 5$

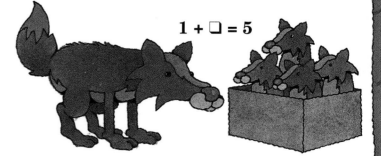

ALLIGATOR, ALLIGATOR! PUT IT ON YOUR CALCULATOR!

MORE FUN. Have your child draw groups of parent and baby animals and write number sentences for each group, using an empty box for each missing number. Ask him or her tell a story for each scene and then to give the missing numbers.

CALCULATOR CODE

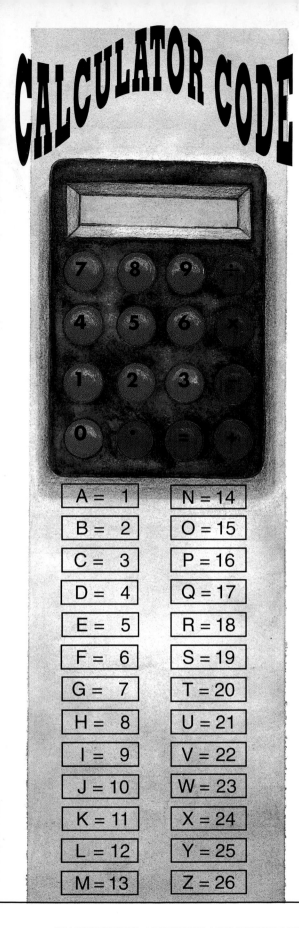

A = 1	N = 14
B = 2	O = 15
C = 3	P = 16
D = 4	Q = 17
E = 5	R = 18
F = 6	S = 19
G = 7	T = 20
H = 8	U = 21
I = 9	V = 22
J = 10	W = 23
K = 11	X = 24
L = 12	Y = 25
M = 13	Z = 26

KANGAROO

How many points is my name worth? First take a guess. Then use your calculator to find out.

**Enter the value of K.
Add the value of A.
Add the value of N.
Keep adding the values of the letters until you have entered the value of the last letter.
Press =.**

Find out exactly how many points my name is worth. Take a guess first, though.

GIRAFFE

**To find the value of the name giraffe, add the values of each letter.
Press =.**

MATH FOCUS: ADDITION AND SUBTRACTION.
By using a calculator to solve problems, children practice addition and subtraction.

Have available a calculator, with large keys if possible. Remind your child to press the + key when adding and the - key when subtracting.

TIGER + ZEBRA

Find the value of the name tiger.
Press +.
Find the value of the name zebra .
Press =.

Take a guess and then check it out!

Are our names worth less than 100 points together or more than 100 points together?

MONKEY-LION

MONKEY-LION

Find the value of the name lion.
Write it on a piece of paper.
Press C.
Do the same for the name monkey.
Enter the larger number on the calculator.
Press –.
Enter the smaller number.
Press =.

Whose name is worth more?

How much more is it worth?

MORE FUN. Make the alphabet code on page 62 reflect dollar amounts and have your child use a calculator to figure out which family member or friend has the most "expensive" name.

ANSWERS. Kangaroo is worth 82 points. Giraffe is worth 52 points. Tiger and Zebra are worth more than 100 points together (111). Monkey (83 points) is worth more than Lion (50 points); Monkey - Lion is 33 points.

TIME-LIFE for CHILDREN™

Publisher: Robert H. Smith
Associate Publisher and Managing Editor: Neil Kagan
Assistant Managing Editor: Patricia Daniels
Editorial Directors: Jean Burke Crawford, Allan Fallow,
   Karin Kinney, Sara Mark, Elizabeth Ward
Director of Marketing: Margaret Mooney
Product Managers: Cassandra Ford,
   Shelley L. Schimkus
Director of Finance: Lisa Peterson
Financial Analyst: Patricia Vanderslice
Administrative Assistant: Barbara A. Jones
Production Manager: Prudence G. Harris
Production: Celia Beattie
Supervisor of Quality Control: James King

Produced by Kirchoff/Wohlberg, Inc.
866 United Nations Plaza,
New York, New York 10017

Series Director: Mary Jane Martin
Creative Director: Morris A. Kirchoff
Mathematics Director: Jo Dennis
Designer: Jessica A. Kirchoff
Assistant Designers: Brian Collins, Mariah Corrigan,
   Ann Eitzen, Judith Schwartz
Contributing Writer: Anne M. Miranda
Managing Editor: Nancy Pernick
Editors: Susan Darwin, Beth Grout, David McCoy

Cover Illustration: Don Madden

Illustration Credits: Diane Blasius, pp. 22–27;
Brian Cody, pp. 60–61; Ron LeHew, pp. 48–59; Don Madden,
pp. 28–37; Carol Nicklaus, pp. 18–21, pp. 40–47;
Andy San Diego, pp. 62–63; Joe Veno, pp. 6–7, pp. 38–39;
John Wallner, pp. 8–17; Fred Winkowski, end papers

Photography Credits: M. Angelo/Westlight, pp. 26–27;
W. Cody/Westlight, pp. 22–25

CONSULTANTS

Mary Jane Martin spent 17 years working in elementary school classrooms as a teacher and reading consultant; for seven of those years she was a first-grade teacher. The second half of her career has been devoted to publishing. During this time she has helped create and produce a wide variety of innovative elementary programs, including two mathematics textbook series.

Jo Dennis has worked as a teacher and math consultant in England, Australia, and the United States for more than 20 years. Most recently, she has helped develop and write several mathematics textbooks for kindergarten, first grade, and second grade.

Catherine Motz Peterson is a curriculum specialist who spent five years developing an early elementary mathematics program for the nationally acclaimed Fairfax County Public Schools in Virginia. She is also mathematics consultant to the University Of Maryland, Catholic University, and the Fredrick County Public Schools in Maryland. Ms. Peterson is the director of the Capitol Hill Day School in Washington, D.C.

First printing. Printed in U.S.A.
Published simultaneously in Canada.

Time Life Inc. is a wholly owned subsidiary of THE TIME INC. BOOK COMPANY

TIME-LIFE is a trademark of Time Warner Inc. U.S.A.

For subscription information, call 1-800-621-7026.

Library of Congress Cataloging-in-Publication Data
The case of the missing zebra stripes: zoo math.
       p.   cm. —— (I love math)
       Summary: A collection of stories, poems, riddles, games, and hands-on activities focusing on the mathematical aspects of a trip to the zoo.
       ISBN 0-8094-9954-1
       1. Mathematics—Juvenile literature. 2. Zoos—Juvenile literature. [1. Mathematics. 2. Mathematical recreations. 3. Zoos—Miscellanea.] I. Time-Life for Children (Firm) II. Series.
QA40.5.C37   1992
510—dc20   92-16838
                                           CIP
                                            AC

Tigers and Turtles

The Number of Players:

2-4

The Object of the Game: To be the first to get to Monkey Island.

The Playing Pieces: A different playing piece for each player—different kinds of coins, for example—and a single die.

The Play: Each player puts a playing piece on START. The youngest player goes first. The play then continues to the right.

Each player throws the die and, according to the number shown, moves his or her playing piece along the path to Monkey Island. If a player lands on a tiger/turtle space, he or she must throw the die again. If the number shown is even, the player moves forward that many spaces. If the number is odd, the player moves back that many spaces.

The Winner: The player who gets to Monkey Island first wins the game. You can get to Monkey Island only if the roll of the die lands you exactly on the bridge.

Math Concepts: Counting 1–6.
Recognition of odd and even numbers.
Multiplication.